Rags to More Than Riches

by

C.A. Chambers

RoseDog Books

PITTSBURGH, PENNSYLVANIA 15222

For additional information or to order additional books, please write:
RoseDog Publishing
701 Smithfield Street
Third Floor
Pittsburgh, Pennsylvania 15222
U.S.A.
1-800-834-1803
Or visit our web site and on-line bookstore at
www.rosedogbookstore.com

To my beloved husband
who loves me through all we go through,
and to the Lord Jesus Christ,
may all of the glory and honor and praise be His,
forever and ever.

Chapter One

What a beautiful day today is. All around you can see the wonders of the Lord. However, there was a time when I could not appreciate the wonderful life that had been given to me. Funny, how we just know our lives are going to be one thing and end up something totally different. My grandfather was a wonderful, spiritual man. He used to always read in the morning and at night. I would watch and wonder sometimes as what he found so interesting. For surely in this great big book he read, there could not be something of importance. He would say, honey whatever you do in this life, follow the Lord and you will be alright. What a profound statement.

Back in the time of growing up I use to think life was so very hard and uncertain. Not knowing why or how things occurred, I became very frustrated. Scared and alone was how I spent most of my years growing up. Abused and beaten, hating life and the Creator that brought me into it. Coming home from school became a nightmare. What was waiting ahead was horrible to me. If things were right, there would be no one home. Otherwise, abuse was waiting. From age 13, I became sexually abused and as a result I became very angry inside. Angry that this could possibly occur and confused as to why it would occur. I would delay coming home to the last possible moment. Wishing the one at home would just die. Praying for it to occur. My mother was at work, clueless as to the events taking place. Scared and being told repeatedly she would not believe anything I said would only get me into more trouble. I would lay in bed doing homework or actually reading this grand book of Papa's. The door opens, in came a man reeking of alcohol and cheap smelling cologne. Fear would grip me and words would sputter out of my mouth in sentences filled with questions, hoping to hold off the inevitable. Hands of enormous size would begin roaming my body. Feeling in places that I had been told was beautiful and designed by God for my husbands pleasure once I was married. Wishing to scream out loud for him to stop and filling with rage inside me. Trying to push off the intrusiveness that was occurring. Minutes seemed like hours, I was wishing for anything. A knock on the door, the phone to ring, something to get this individual off of me and to stop exploring my body. Day after day, week after week, this would take place. I cursed the day of being born, wishing I would just die. Feelings of no self worth began to immerge. If resistance were offered, slaps would ensue. Slaps filled with hate and control. Words spoken of degrade and malice. Why were men abusive? Beatings on my mother occurred. Drunkenness was a norm. Although he would not consider this as such, that was all he would consume. I still smell the reek of him and hear the hate filled words that were filling the air as I was growing up in what some would consider a "normal " household. What have I done to deserve such a terrible experience? Why would a wonderful creator allow this horrible thing to occur? Was there a God out there caring and loving each one of us like my grandfather had often stated? Was there a divine purpose for this? I would not begin to find out this answer until many years later.

Escape was a process of relieving these feelings. Denial and bitterness consumed my life. I have so much emptiness. How can the world around me continue on the path with everyone so engrossed with their life, they could not see what is going on around them. I began to curse and live recklessly. Men I would meet through my friends would have the same look in their eyes. Lusting after what seemed to be alright to have. To possess and destroy. Not caring what damage occurred to the inno-cent, mentally or physically. Friend's brothers would suggest they were interested in getting to know me. Starving for some-one to care for me from the male persuasion in a proper way, I fell into their ploys. Finally deciding this was not the great gift of God, this body of mine, its purpose must be for men's pleas-ure. Even if it was at my expense. All I knew was pain and hurt came from men. Rage still filled my heart. Hatred for men became my past time. I would sit and envision how I could see the way I wished men would die. I could not take it anymore and left home at sixteen, breaking my mothers' heart and wor-rying her completely. Staying at home and going through the process I had to endure was no longer an option for me. My feeling of freedom was around the corner. How wonderful...to know happiness was soon to come. I packed my belongings and moved out of the location I had grown up in. Leaving behind, bittersweet memories. Cutting all ties with my mom. Blaming her for events that had occurred and telling her it was because I could not live under her rules any longer. Never sharing the hurt, anger and bitterness inside.

Moving to a big city had all of the excitement of going into another world. The buildings were as huge as mountains to me. Opportunities awaited me. I was a young woman in a growing city. Life began to come together. I met new friends and began to live again. I was inspired to become creative and explore the new world around me. Determined to leave my past and all of its painful experiences behind me, I pushed down all of the feelings I had endured. I was hardened and calloused ready for a new job and a new way of life. By age eighteen I had experienced enough hurt for a lifetime. Relationships were abusive and on a ride that would take my fairy tale world and spiral it into a living hell on earth.

Chapter Two

Opportunity to make money quickly seemed to be an answer. Money would resolve all of these problems. Men would appreciate me for what I had. Events in life would change and I would be somebody. Someone to love. Someone to give love even if this world was not willing to return it. During this process, I met a couple who were very involved in the church and the "God" thing. They would pray together, worship together and most of all they seemed happy. Genuinely happy. They did not make a lot of money but they seemed content. Four children and the father was the only one working and surprisingly making ends meet. The mother stayed home with all of the children. I will always remember seeing her playing and loving them. Reading this great big book my grandfather use to read. Smiling and talking to herself as she read. What a mystery. I knew God, I knew how to read this book, but whatever she had I longed for. Children fussing and playing about, she seemed to not mind and in fact to enjoy this time in her life. I looked at myself, low self esteem, grumpy, feeling terribly depressed and desperate for a change. In a city with no true friends, at least no one who would certainly understand what I was feeling, wishing to have that happiness. I could not call home, that would admit defeat. I was not defeated by any means. Just a little set back. I could be like this woman, content and happy, capable of giving love. To be with someone. Just to express and have in return what I was witnessing. A new man emerged in my life. One, who on the outside had the appearance of a knight in shining armor. But inside, one whose temper seemed for some reason to rise daily. Fist would slam through walls and doors. Destroying things. Destroying me. Images of growing up arose again. Thoughts left long ago, rising to the occasion. Being told, " I love you" in one breath and degrading you in another. Words making you feel as if you wished you were six feet under the ground. Crying inside for some type of answer. Wanting and pleading with myself to seek help only to know pride would come and take away that avenue. My world was falling apart fast and I needed to fix it quickly. The sooner the better for the path I was taking was going to destroy me faster than I knew.

Parties and nightclubs, an atmosphere to desire, or so I thought. People and places to discover. Islands and resorts to visit. My mind filling with fairy tale images. Only to find out what I would discover would be a world all of its own. Ethics and codes of cultures no one speaks about. I was determined, if I manipulate enough, I can conquer this world and all of its evil vices. People seek pleasure in any form that will be made available to them. Our bodies only to be used and then tossed aside as waste. Mentally, we starve as we try to figure out the one thing we need is the farthest possession from our grasp. People laying around, needles in their arms. Crying for more, just to experience this hell all over again. Bloodied faces and bodies. Beaten and cut, instructed not ever again to try and undermine the authority that is now over them. Where to go and what to do? Too scared to move only waiting for the controller to leave and allow some type of comfort. If only momentarily. Visions of this fill movie theatres and novels. But I am here to share with you the reality of such a life.

When you are alone you become desperate. Reasons for things do not seem to make sense. Decisions become obscured and your vision in life definitely becomes overwhelming to say the least. People come around and make themselves available to you for their pleasure. Only their pleasure. Life becomes a maze of images and confusion sets in. Thinking the whole while, I am going to be worth something. Something important. Because, deep down in my heart I hear the words of my Papa saying,"God did not make junk and I was a special creation." Try as I might, life did not change. Arguments ensued, violence erupted. My hell on earth was beginning to spiral downward faster and faster. The fast life and experiences were coming close to an end. The one relationship I had built was awful and cruel. Statements of hate were exchanged. How I longed to talk with someone to answer my questions. Hearts breaking and lives changing could not seem more difficult than now. Life, as it was suppose to be, was no more. Parties full of people with persuasive ways and speech. All the upbringing in the world had not prepared me for what was going to occur.

You can be beaten, battered and torn in all directions and still deny you are choosing the path of destruction. Sometimes you MUST hit bottom first. Although life was difficult Jesus was still there. Planting people and opportunities for me to grasp. Still allowing me to hear those precious words from Papa. Marie came into my life with her husband. They were members of a church and were inviting me to attend. Planting a seed of faith and allowing it to prosper in time. I began to attend. Messages of old seem to resurface. Some confusion still lingered on all of the events that had transpired. Relationships broken from home to the near and dear. Having no one to turn to; where would I go? Home? No! Never! The defeat issue again. I could never do that. What would people think?

So turning my back on God, I was off again, to venture into a place where satan preys on the weak. Moving back to my hometown but still not communicating with my mother, I began to find ties could not be broken with the life I had just come from. Calls in the night from people I was wishing to forget. Turning once again to the previous relationship with my "knight in shinning armor." Placing my heart once again out there for it to be held and loved. Comforted from the storm which I had already endured. Wanting so desperately to be free of pain and sorrow. Holding firm to the only thing I had left. Coming to him with my tearful eyes hoping against hope we both could make the relationship workout. Memories of the hateful words and destroying battles were pushed far beneath the surface. I could endure it. He would change and I would be there by his side. Awaiting for the love to come and compassion to encompass me. Swallowing me up, sending me into my fairy tale world. Days began in bliss. Kind and caring words were spoken. Promises of change. Tempers seemed to diminish. Possibly this was my knight in shinning armor. Still with all of this in my life, something was missing. The joy and contentment I remember seeing in some of the peoples lives that had crossed my path was not here for the taking.

Thoughts about Jesus began to enter into my mind. Maybe if I take time to pray things will be better. Besides, a quick prayer will not hurt. People in desperate situations have to do desperate things. This was desperate. Confusion began to set in. For the more I prayed for change, the more things changed. For the worse. The fighting began again. As I lay in bed next to the man I loved, coldness would flow from his being. I would lay next to this warm breathing body wanting to be held. Wishing the love I had seen in others relationship would flow from ours. Our most intimate moments would be predictable. Unhappiness set in and feelings of inadequacy overwhelmed me. Reminders of how men were and how they abused the privilege of knowing a woman. What should have been loving moments were suffering for me. I did not want to feel hands on my body. I knew in my heart I did not love him any longer. There was too much damage and this night was not going to take place. Tempers flared to the maximum. What had started in a kind gesture turned into one of disgust. Holding me down seemed to excite him even more. The more I struggled the more forceful he became. Finally after battling in my mind the consequences as to this altercation, I was determined not to be taken again against my will. Enough of this had occurred and no longer was it going to. Enraged, as we said things of hatred, I reached for the phone to call the police. Threats came out of his mouth and the phone was ripped out of the wall and thrown across the room. Advances in rage were made and I vowed then to never be in this circumstance again, or to allow anyone to hurt me. I had to do something. Jesus had to be the answer. He was the only one person who would always be there for me to turn to.

Many years have passed since this time in my life. Wondering through life with what seems to be an endless search for this feeling of peace. Still continuing in the church, messages would be preached and there I would sit and listen. Taking every word into mind and wondering if anyone had ever had the experiences of hurt I had gone through. Yes, there is one who has experienced this: JESUS.

Sometimes we forget the obvious. We forget there is a Master of this universe and a Creator who has loved us since before we were formed. I have finally come to peace within myself. But to have accomplished this, I must share with you a little more of my life. God has blessed me so. He will bless you also. You must remain patient and follow His commands. Soon as you finish this book, you will begin to understand that Jesus did die for you and me. He gave up His life for us. The heavenly father, which we were created by, does have a magnificent plan for you. He is with you during all of your hurts and sorrows. Allowing this to occur for you to become a vessel for his use once you commit your life to him.

After a painful divorce and recovery from years of abuse, I began to realize through experiences that I have to take hold and do something with my life. No one is going to hand me things just because I am a breathing being. Decisions need to be made for a positive outcome in your life. For years, I could not understand the reason I still was not happy. Things were going good and seemed to be alright. Why wasn't I experiencing the peace that the people of my past had? I would go to church. I would pray. But dear one, if you do all of this in the pretense things will be fine, you are fooling yourself. You must give of yourself **totally** to Christ. No holds barred.

I am here today by the grace of God. For the remainder of this book, I would like for you to go on a journey with me. Together we will find this wonderful Savior of ours and begin to understand how He wants us to live. It is not so far fetched, not so out of reach. Come travel with me and I will share with you the reality of what a peaceful and blessed life we were given. Please do not cheat yourself by not following some of the exercises suggested. You will see at the end how they will benefit you.

Chapter Three

First of all, perhaps, some of you may not really know what salvation is. So look with me at the following verses in your Bible. John 3:16 says, For God so loved the world He gave His only begotten son, that whoever believes in him shall not perish but have eternal life.

God so loved us... miserable, wretched, broken and battered; that he gave his ONLY son to die for us. Redeeming us from all inequities and infirmities.

Romans 4: 24 and 25 says, also for us, to whom God will credit righteousness, for us who believe in him who raised Jesus our Lord from the dead. He was delivered over to death for our sins and was raised to life for our justification. Now you may be saying Cheryl, I am far from righteousness. Beloved you are there. You were there in righteousness the moment you accepted the Lord Jesus into your heart and gave your life to him completely. There is NO sin or circumstance that Jesus does not have the answer for.

Let's continue. Please take time and read, Romans chapter 6. Read it slow and understand what it is saying. We were buried with him through baptism into death in order that just as Christ was raised from the dead through the glory of the Father, we too may live a new life.

You, my friend, have become a new creation in Christ. (II Cor. 5:17) Allow the Holy Spirit to speak to you. ALL THE OLD HAS GONE, the new has come. Do you hear this. No matter what the circumstance, how bad you feel the sin is, how unworthy you think you are. He has died for you. Life changing occurrences are going to take place. Why? Because God foreknew you before birth. He finds pleasure in you. Isn't that wonderful, he finds pleasure in us. Let's take a brief journey through the Bible and see what it says of His pleasure in us.

Lets look at Psalms 115:3. Our God is in heaven; he does whatever pleases him. Stop and think about this a moment. He chose to save us because it pleases him. Ephesians 1:4. For he chose us in him before the creation of the world to be holy and blameless in his sight. In love he predestined us to be adopted as his sons through Jesus Christ, in accordance with his pleasure and will...These are just a couple of scriptures pertaining to this. Research your bible after this study and find for yourself how God pleases in you. For if you research for yourself you begin to understand just how precious you are to your heavenly father. Let's move on.

First we know Christ died for us and our sins. Now we have a decision to make. It will not be an easy one. But it is an important one. Are you willing to give yourself totally to God? Completely? Allowing all of the hidden doors in your heart to be opened? If so, lets journey further. God has placed a prayer in my heart for you as I write this. Please, let's pray together.

Father, most merciful one, purge our hearts, search them for any unrighteousness. Father, forgive me of my sins. I pour my heart to you, seeking you earnestly. Knocking as you say to do in obedience with scripture. Awaiting for you to come and heal my wounds. We proclaim Jer. 17:14, Heal me O Lord, and I will be healed: save me O Lord, and I will be saved. Lord, we confess with our mouths you are Lord. King of Kings. Fill me father with the Holy Spirit. Give me discernment. Lead my path. Thank you Jesus for dying for me. In your sweet precious name we pray. Amen.

Great! Let's go forward. The first step, as I mentioned is change. You have a choice to do this. It begins with a decision. You have completed that process. You have accepted Christ as your master. You may be saying.. Cheryl, I have sinned after I was saved or this hurt occurred after accepting Christ. For you, we have to stand on I John 1:9.

As the Holy Spirit begins to work within you the devil will attack you even more. Remember Jesus in the wilderness. Satan tempted him. Why? He went to pray and fast. What does it say? Jesus quoted scripture to satan but he persisted until He commanded him to be gone. He did not give up after one or two tries. This is why it is so very important that you engulf yourself in Gods word. The last thing satan wants is for you to become close to your heavenly father. He (the devil) knows what a victorious life you will have. Remember he used to be an angel and was cast down. He knows Gods word, so we better know Gods word.

Lets look at the book of Philippians. Chapter 3:12. You have already made your decision to change. So let's see how to do that. Not that I have already obtained all this, or have already been made perfect, but I press on to take hold of that for which Christ took hold of me. But one thing I do: Forgetting what is behind and straining toward what is ahead. I press on toward the goal to win the prize for which God has called me, heavenward in Christ Jesus. Paul, of all people, understood what it is to leave behind the old self. He had persecuted God's people for many years. Now he is a powerful, spirit filled disciple. Forgetting what is behind. God says he forgets our sin as far from the east to the west. Should we not forget it also and quit battering ourselves with the past sins? When you focus on this instead of what is ahead, you are allowing satan victory over your thoughts. Phil. 4:8 says we are to think on things that are pure, true, noble, right, lovely, admirable, excellent or praiseworthy. If your thoughts are not in alignment with this, guess what? They are not from God. Therefore pray and rid yourself of these things. Since you have been justified through faith, we have peace with God through our Lord Jesus through whom we have gained access by faith into this grace which we now stand. Rejoice in the hope of the glory of God. Not, only so, but we also rejoice in our sufferings, because they produce perseverance, character, hope and hope does not disappoint us. God has poured out his love into our hearts by the Holy Spirit, whom he has given us. (my paraphrasing) Well isn't that something. Now we are forgiven and justified through Christ. (grace) We have peace with God. Lets continue to see what the scripture says on grace.

Rom. 3: 22, this righteousness from God comes through faith in Jesus to all who believe. There is no difference for all have sinned and fallen short of the glory of god, and are justified freely by his grace through the redemption that came by Christ Jesus. God presented him as a sacrifice of atonement, through faith in his blood. Ephesians 1:10-13, In him we have redemption through his blood, the forgiveness of sins, in accordance with the riches of God's grace which he lavished on us with all wisdom and understanding... we were chosen having been predestined according to the plan of him who works out everything in conformity with the purpose of his will... in Christ, might be for the praise of his glory. You were included in Christ when you heard the word of truth. The gospel of your salvation.

Chapter Four

Now we have to trust. Without trust in God, you can't take him at his word. If you can't believe what he has written, then you are denying yourself of a miracle healing. Where else can we experience the cleansing power of the blood of the Lamb. He is our healer, our all. If you have researched the scriptures as I asked and see how God loves you so very much, how can you look else where for healing? You might say, well mine is not physical, it is emotional or mental. Are you willing to compromise God for mere man? Who is our creator! God made man in His image. We are to trust and turn to God no matter what the circumstance. Good or bad. We have to put our hope in Him. The author and finisher of all. When we are at our wits end where will we place our hope? Lets look at

Psalms 42 and 43. Read it slow and mark the answers to the following questions.

1. Where do we go when you are depressed or downcast?

2. When you are disturbed within yourself, what do you do?

3. Who is your stronghold?

Do you see a connection here? Where are we to turn? Look at Psalms 119. I know it is long, but read it after you finish the above Psalms. Look at the parallel between them. Hope, life, guidance, wisdom and discernment are all there awaiting for you to grasp and cherish.

Look at Psalms 121, what a wonderful promise from God. We could continue to research on and on with this issue. But again the bottom line is trust. It is your responsibility to trust the Loving God that created you. The Alpha and Omega. Satan has kept you captive all of these years, won't you give Jesus a chance?

I am not going to say some things will automatically pass away. Some will and some won't. But as believers we have to know Gods grace is sufficient for me and He is my Lord. He will continue to convict and heal you in all areas of your life during your walk with him. Remember once you were alienated from

God and were enemies in your minds because of your evil behavior. Now he has reconciled you by Christ's physical body through death to present you holy in his sight, without blemish and free from accusation. If you have the faith as small as a mustard seed, you can say to this mountain move and it shall do so. (my quote)

Remember, take these truths and apply them. Forgive those who have hurt you. One of my deepest hurts was one that I clung to the longest. What a wonderful joy it was when I finally gave it to Jesus. It was not until I realized you can hate the sin, but love the sinner in Christ. Look at II Cor. 10:7 and 5:16. What is the parallel? We can not look at things from a worldly point of view any longer. So make the decision to separate the two and follow Christ's teaching on forgiveness. You will be so blessed.

I close this book with the following scripture. May God richly bless you as you journey through your life, keeping Him first with all you do.

He who dwells in the shelter of the Most High will rest in the shadow of the Almighty. I will say of the Lord, He is my refuge and my fortress, my God in whom I trust. Surely he will save you from the fowler's snare and from the deadly pestilence. He will cover you with his feathers and under his wings you will find refuge, his faithfulness will be your shield and rampart. You will not fear the terror of night, nor the arrow that flies by day, nor the pestilence that stalks in the darkness, nor the plague that destroys at midday. A thousand may fall at your side, ten thousand at your right hand, but it will not come near you. You will only observe with your eyes and see the punishment of the wicked. If you make the Most High your dwelling, even the Lord who is my refuge, then no harm will befall you, no disaster will come near your tent. For he will command his angels concerning you to guard you in all your ways. They will lift you up in their hands, so you will not strike your foot against a stone. You will tread upon the lion and the cobra, you will trample the great lion and serpent. Because he loves me, says the Lord I will rescue him, I will protect him for he acknowledges my name. He will call upon me, and I will answer him, I will be with him in trouble and deliver him and honor him. With long life, will I satisfy him and show him salvation.

May God be the glory for giving me the inspiration for this book.

God has blessed me with a wonderful, spirit filled husband, who understands me more than I could ever imagine. He is filled with Gods love and has a love for me as Christ loved the church. Thank you, Jesus, for providing me with happiness and peace. Praise be to your name forever.